Tuba

# RODGERS & HAMMERSTEIN HITS

arranged for brass quintet
by Charles Sayre

*easy level*

THE CANADIAN
BRASS

C A N A D I A N
B R A S S
SERIES OF
COLLECTED QUINTETS

HAL•LEONARD®
CORPORATION
7777 W. BLUEMOUND RD. P.O. BOX 13819 MILWAUKEE, WI 53213

# C A N A D I A N
# B R A S S
## SERIES OF
## COLLECTED QUINTETS

# RODGERS &
# HAMMERSTEIN HITS

## arranged for brass quintet
## by Charles Sayre

## contents

3 **Blow High, Blow Low**
   from *Carousel*

4 **Edelweiss**
   from *The Sound of Music*

5 **Honey Bun**
   from *South Pacific*

6 **Oh, What a Beautiful Mornin'**
   from *Oklahoma!*

7 **Oklahoma**
   from *Oklahoma!*

8 **You'll Never Walk Alone**
   from *Carousel*

Welcome to the new *Canadian Brass Series of Collected Quintets.* In our work with students we have for some time been aware of the need for more brass quintet music at easy and intermediate levels of difficulty. We are continually observing a kind of "Renaissance" in brass music, not only in audience responses to our quintet, but to all brass music in general. The brass quintet, as a chamber ensemble, seems to have become as standard a chamber combination as a string quartet. That could not have been said twenty-five years ago. Brass quintets are popping up everywhere — professional quintets, junior and senior high school ensembles, college and university groups, and amateur quintets of adult players.

We have carefully chosen the literature for these collected quintets, and closely supervised the arrangements. Our aim was to retain a Canadian Brass flavor to each arrangement, and create attractive repertory designed so that any brass quintet can play it with satisfying results. We've often remarked to one another that we certainly wish that we'd had quintet arrangements like these when we were students!

Happy playing to you and your quintet.

— THE CANADIAN BRASS

# BLOW HIGH, BLOW LOW
## (From "CAROUSEL")

3

Lyrics by Oscar Hammerstein II
Music by Richard Rodgers

TUBA

# EDELWEISS
## (From "THE SOUND OF MUSIC")

TUBA

Lyrics by Oscar Hammerstein II
Music by Richard Rodgers

# HONEY BUN
## From ("South Pacific")

TUBA

Lyrics by Oscar Hammerstein II
Music by Richard Rodgers

# OH, WHAT A BEAUTIFUL MORNIN'

(From "OKLAHOMA!")

TUBA

Lyrics by Oscar Hammerstein II
Music by Richard Rodgers

# OKLAHOMA
### (From "OKLAHOMA!")

TUBA

Lyrics by Oscar Hammerstein II
Music by Richard Rodgers

# YOU'LL NEVER WALK ALONE
## (From "CAROUSEL")

**TUBA**

Lyrics by Oscar Hammerstein II
Music by Richard Rodgers

*Legato phrasing throughout

ISBN-13: 978-1-4584-0164-9

Distributed By
HAL LEONARD

HL50488770
U.S. 8.99

50488770

0 73999 58705 0

9 781458 401649